Project Hippopotamus

Susan Ring

Weigl Publishers Inc.

Editor
Diana Marshall

Design and Layout
Warren Clark
Bryan Pezzi

Copy Editor
Heather Kissock

Photo Researcher
Tina Schwartzenberger

DEVELOPED IN COLLABORATION WITH THE TOLEDO ZOO

The publisher wishes
to thank Andi Norman
and Steve Krueger
for their assistance.

Published by Weigl Publishers Inc.
123 South Broad Street, Box 227
Mankato, MN 56002 USA
Web site: www.weigl.com

Library of Congress Cataloging-in-Publication Data

Ring, Susan.
 Project hippopotamusnew / Susan Ring.
 p. cm. -- (Zoo life)
Summary: Showcases the development and growth of a baby hippopotamus at
a zoo, discussing the zookeeper's role in its life and the natural
habitat, foods, and life cycle of the animal.
 ISBN 1-59036-013-3 (lib. bdg. : alk. paper)
 1. Hippopotamus--Infancy--Juvenile literature. 2. Zoo
animals--Ohio--Toledo--Juvenile literature. [1. Hippopotamus. 2.
Animals--Infancy. 3. Zoo animals.] I. Title. II. Zoo babies (Mankato,
Minn.)
 QL737.U57 R56 2002
 599.63'5139--dc21

 2002006393

Printed in the United States of America
1 2 3 4 5 6 7 8 9 0   06 05 04 03 02

Photograph Credits
Every reasonable effort has been made to trace ownership and to obtain permission to reprint
copyright material. The publishers would be pleased to have any errors or omissions brought
to their attention so that they may be corrected in subsequent printings.
Cover: baby hippopotamus (© Linda S. Milks/The Toledo Zoo); **Corel Corporation:** pages 21, 22
bottom; **Bill Everitt/Tom Stack & Associates:** page 17 right; **D. Robert Franz:** pages 17 left, 19, 20;
Joe McDonald/Tom Stack & Associates: pages 9, 18; © **Linda S. Milks/The Toledo Zoo:** title page,
pages 3, 4, 5, 6, 7, 8, 10, 11, 12, 13, 14, 17 far right; **Mark Newman/Tom Stack & Associates:** pages
16, 23; **Courtesy of The Toledo Zoo:** pages 15, 17 far left, 22 top.

Contents

A Baby is Born

The Toledo Zoo welcomed a new member to its animal family at about 11 o'clock one morning. A baby hippopotamus was born early in August. The 85-pound baby was born underwater. Water is a safe place for a hippo to be born. Still, the first thing the baby had to do was come up to the water's surface for air.

Zoo Issues

Should newborn baby animals be put on public display?

The newborn hippo looked like a small adult. He was skinnier, and his head was more round.

- A baby hippo is called a calf.

- The word hippopotamus means "river horse" in the Latin language. This name suits the hippo, which lives in or near rivers and streams.

- When baby hippos nurse, their ears fold over and their nostrils close. This stops water from entering their ears and nose when they nurse underwater.

- In the wild, baby hippos are born during the rainy season. There is plenty of grass to eat during rainy seasons. In zoos, hippos are born year-round.

Like all baby hippos, he was born with his eyes open. He was also born with the **instinct** to nurse, or drink his mother's milk. He tried to nurse within the first hour. He was not successful until almost 8 hours after being born.

Only 3 hours after being born, the newborn left the water and stood on land. One hour after that, he began to walk around.

It was a happy sight when the baby hippo found the milk he needed.

Meet the Baby

When **zookeepers** at The Toledo Zoo decided that it was time to name the baby, they took a vote. The zookeepers chose the name Herbie the Herbivore. A herbivore is an animal that only eats plants.

Zoo Issues

Should baby zoo animals share exhibits with their mother? Why?

Herbie's teeth will soon be long and sharp. Still, he will never eat meat.

Herbie was born knowing how to come up to the water's surface for air. Still, his mother had to show him when to go for air. She guided him to the water's surface. From her, Herbie learned to push off the bottom of the pool. She taught him to avoid the deep water. Herbie's mother also taught him how to act with the other hippopotamuses in the **exhibit**. At first, Herbie stayed very close to his mother.

BRAIN BOOSTERS

- Thousands of years ago, hippo **habitats** could be found in Africa, Asia, and Europe. Now, hippos are found only in Africa. They live south of the Sahara desert, wherever water and grasslands are found. Hippos stay cool in streams and rivers. They feed off the grasslands.

- There are two kinds of hippos. They are the river hippopotamus and the pygmy hippopotamus. Herbie is a river hippo.

- In 1987, The Toledo Zoo became the first zoo in the world to record an underwater hippo birth on video camera.

When the water was too deep for him to stand in, Herbie's mother let him climb onto her back so that she could carry him across the pool.

Wet and Wild

Hippos do not really swim or float. Instead, they push off the bottom of rivers or pools and leap from place to place underwater. Once Herbie learned how to move under the water's surface, he looked like an underwater ballet dancer. He loved rolling over and over on his side in the water. Called a barrel roll, Herbie likely learned this skill from his mother. She also enjoys barrel rolls. Herbie and his mother do them often.

Zoo Issues

Why should zoo exhibits be similar to an animal's natural habitat?

Before long, Herbie was moving about the water with ease.

- A newborn hippopotamus weighs between 50 and 120 pounds.

- Hippos reach their adult size at about 5 years of age. Adult hippos can weigh 3 to 4 tons. They can grow to be 10 to 13 feet long and about 5 feet tall.

- Hippo calves drink their mother's milk for about 8 months. Sometimes, a mother hippo will let her baby nurse slightly longer. When they are about 4 weeks old, hippo calves begin to eat grass as well. Serious **grazing** begins at about 4 months of age.

Like hippos in the wild, young Herbie was most active in the late afternoon. He liked to play with a 2.5-foot boomer ball. He would come out of the water, push the ball up, toss it, chase it, and bite it. This fun exercise helped keep the baby hippo active and fit.

Hippos can be **aggressive**. Herbie is very friendly compared to most hippos. He is also curious. Herbie often rests his head on cables between the hippopotamus and elephant pools to watch the elephants play.

Meet the Parents

Herbie is Emma's first baby.

Herbie's mother is named Emma. Emma was born in 1995 at Colorado's Denver Zoo. Cupid, Herbie's father, was born around 1954. Zookeepers believe that Cupid was born in the wild. At that time, zoos did not keep records, so his exact date of birth is not known. Herbie is Cupid's fourteenth baby.

Zoo Issues

Think of some reasons why zoo animals may need to be separated.

- Female hippopotamuses are ready to mate at about 5 to 9 years of age. Male hippos are ready to mate between 7 and 12 years of age.

- Female hippos do not usually fight, but a mother will viciously fight to defend her baby.

- The hippopotamus is the second-largest land animal. Only the elephant weighs more than the hippo.

- Male hippos mark their **territory**. They wag their tails quickly to spread their **dung** along the riverbanks.

- Often, hippo calves live with their mother until they are fully grown. A mother may have regular contact with four of her young at one time.

Emma and Cupid were introduced when Emma was 10 months old. They liked each other right away. They lived together for almost 4 years before Emma gave birth to Herbie. About 1 month after Herbie was born, Emma and Cupid were separated. The zookeepers did not want them to produce another baby. Now, Emma and Herbie live together in one of the indoor stalls. Cupid lives in a separate stall with Bubbles, another female hippo.

■ The Toledo Zoo's outside exhibit is called the Hippoquarium. Emma and Herbie take turns with Cupid and Bubbles spending time in the Hippoquarium.

The Zoo Crew

In the wild, hippos graze at night to avoid predators and the hot sun. The zookeepers at The Toledo Zoo feed the hippos twice during the day. This allows them to check the hippos for injuries or illnesses. Using treats, such as apples and bananas, the hippos have been trained to lift a foot, open their mouth, or move from one stall to another. Zookeepers make sure the hippos are healthy. Food is brought into the dry stalls inside. The hippos are fed hay and grain pellets.

■ The hippos' exhibit copies their natural habitat. It includes sloped riverbanks that lead to water and hanging tree branches that hippos can eat.

Zookeepers provide balls, toys, and other objects that keep the hippos interested and active. They clean the exhibit. They also weigh the hippos, which is not an easy task. The zoo's **veterinarians** give the hippopotamuses regular checkups and **vaccines**, as well as medicines when they are sick.

Viewing areas let zoo visitors watch the hippos go about their daily lives underwater.

HOW DO I BECOME A DOCENT?

Docents are volunteer educators who work at zoos. They teach visitors about animal behavior and **conservation** issues. Docents must be at least 18 years old and love animals. They must also take a training course offered by the zoos. Start learning about animals by reading about them. Contact your local zoo to find out about summer schools.

ZOO RULES

The Toledo Zoo's Hippoquarium was the first of its kind in the world. This large, modern exhibit is filled with 360,000 gallons of clean water. Visitors can go right up to the glass to get a close look at the hippos' underwater world. This is the hippos' home and should be respected. Zoos have special rules that help keep animals and visitors safe and healthy.

The Toledo Zoo's Rules:
1. Do not bang on the glass.
2. Do not throw anything into the water.
3. Do not feed the animals.

Animal Gear

It is hard to miss a hippopotamus. The water-loving animal has a round body, little ears, and bulging eyes. These features, along with several others, help hippos live in the lakes and rivers of Africa.

Zoo Issues

Why is it important for zoo food to be similar to animals' food in the wild?

Eyes, Ears, and Nose

The eyes, ears, and nose are located on the top half of a hippo's head. When a hippo is **submerged**, its eyes, ears, and nose remain visible above the surface. This allows a hippo to hide underwater and still be alert to animals or events on land. Their nostrils and ears close when hippos move underwater.

Skin

Long ago, people believed that hippos sweat blood. This is not true. A pink-colored liquid oozes out of their skin. The liquid is a natural sunscreen. It protects hippos' sensitive skin from the hot African sun. Since the hippo has very little hair, the liquid may also protect against skin infections.

Teeth

After whales, hippos have the second-largest mouth of all **mammals**. Flat teeth at the back of their mouths are used for grinding food. Their long **incisors** and **canine teeth** are tusks. Hippos use their tusks to protect themselves in fights. When hippos bite, their upper and lower teeth meet and can cut like a pair of scissors.

Feet and Legs

Hippos have strong legs and feet to hold their weight. They have four hoof-tipped toes. On land, their toes spread apart to give the hippos good balance. Hippo feet are slightly webbed to help them move easily through the water.

In the Wild

River hippopotamuses travel across the African **savanna** in search of food. They may walk up to 5 miles a night. They can eat about 150 pounds of grass in one night. In the water, they form groups called herds. One herd may consist of between five and ninety members. Females take care of the young. Males defend the territory.

Hippos stay out of the sun to keep themselves cool. They spend days in the water. Once the sun sets and the temperature cools, hippos leave the water to graze.

Hippos spend most of the daytime crowding into rivers or lakes. Resting in the water helps support their weight.

These water-loving giants are very helpful to other animals that share their home in the African savanna. Their feet stir up the mud at the bottom of lakes and rivers. This brings small creatures up to the surface for fish to eat. Their dung provides food for tiny plants. Sometimes, fish swim into hippos' mouths searching for food stuck in their teeth.

BRAIN BOOSTERS

- Brutal fights happen between males over territory. A male hippo may guard a herd for weeks, months, or years.

- Hippos often remain under the water's surface for 5 minutes at a time. Hippos fall asleep underwater, raising their heads for air once a minute.

- Hippos have special lips for grazing. In the wild, an area grazed by hippopotamuses looks like it has been mowed. It is called a "hippo lawn."

Some types of birds pick and eat insects off hippopotamuses' skin. They even rest on hippos' backs.

Hippos and Humans

Mother hippopotamuses protect their young from natural predators, such as lions, hyenas, and crocodiles, but humans are the hippo's worst enemy. Humans have destroyed much hippo habitat to build towns and cities. Hippo hunting is still common in parts of Africa. Hippos are hunted for their tusks, which are made of **ivory**. The ivory is used to make jewelry and carvings, which are then sold.

Zoo Issues

How can zoos help wild animal populations?

The savanna grasslands are being destroyed to make room for farmland.

Wildlife reserves in Africa have been created to protect hippos from habitat loss and hunting. In zoos, hippos are free from dangers, such as predators, diseases, hunters, and habitat loss. They receive regular medical care and have plenty of food. Zoos help educate people about hippopotamuses. In zoos, people can watch hippos up close and appreciate their underwater lifestyle.

■ Learning about hippos in zoos will help the wild hippopotamus population's chance of survival.

Hippo Issues

Benefits of Zoo Life

- No danger from predators, hunting, competition, or habitat loss
- Regular food, play time, and medical care
- Can help educate the public about hippos
- Is easier to research hippos in zoos
- Breeding programs maintain a stable zoo population
- Can live a longer life

Benefits of Life in the Wild

- More natural space in which to feed and live
- Maintain diverse hippopotamus populations
- Daily mental and physical challenges, such as finding food
- Part of the natural web of life consisting of plants, predators, and prey
- Live complex lives
- Maintain independence

Folk Tale

Why the Hippo is So Ugly

A long time ago, hippopotamuses had silky hair, long flowing tails, and long ears. Hippo spent most of his time looking at his own reflection in the water. Rabbit, who was tired of listening to Hippo brag, tricked him into sleeping on a soft bed of grass, which Rabbit set on fire. Hippo awoke to discover that he had no hair, and his ears and tail had shrunk. From that day forward, hippos remained underwater to hide. They only come out at night when no one can see them.

Source: Tulin, Melissa S. *Aardvarks to Zebras*. New York: Citadel Press, 1994.

More Information

The Internet can lead you to some exciting information on hippopotamuses. Try searching on your own, or visit the following Web sites:

American Zoo and Aquarium Association (AZA)
www.aza.org

National Geographic Creature Feature
www.nationalgeographic.com/kids/creature_feature/
0009/hippos2.html

The Toledo Zoo www.toledozoo.org

The World Conservation Union Hippo Specialty Group
moray.ml.duke.edu/projects/hippos

CONSERVATION GROUPS

There are many organizations involved in hippo research and conservation. You can get information on hippopotamuses by writing to the following addresses:

INTERNATIONAL
International Fund for
Animal Welfare
P.O. Box 193
411 Main Street
Yarmouth Port, MA 02675
USA

UNITED STATES
African Wildlife Foundation
U.S. Office
1400 16th Street NW
Suite 120
Washington, DC 20036

Words to Know

aggressive: forceful and protective

bonding: forming a close relationship

breeding program: producing babies by mating selected animals

canine teeth: the long, pointed teeth toward the front of the mouth

captivity: kept in an exhibit; not in the wild

conservation: the care and monitoring of animals and animal populations for their continued existence

crèche: a group of mothers and their calves in a protected area

dung: animals' waste matter

exhibit: a space on display that looks similar to an animal's natural habitat

grazing: feeding on grass

habitat: place in the wild where an animal naturally lives

incisors: large, sharp front teeth

instinct: something an animal knows naturally, without being taught

ivory: hard, white material that makes up a hippo's tusks

mammals: warm-blooded animals

predators: animals that hunt and kill other animals for food

savanna: wide, open grasslands in Africa

submerged: under the water's surface

territory: area that an animal will defend as its own

vaccines: medicines that are given to prevent diseases

veterinarians: animal doctors

wildlife reserves: areas of land set apart to protect animals in danger

zookeepers: people at a zoo who feed and take care of the animals

Index